THE TANGO GUITAR TECHNIQUE BOOK

Master the Art of Rhythm, Harmony, & Improvisation for Tango Guitar

DARYL KELLIE

FUNDAMENTAL CHANGES

The Tango Guitar Technique Book

Master the Art of Rhythm, Harmony, & Improvisation for Tango Guitar

ISBN: 978-1-78933-459-3

Published by www.fundamental-changes.com

Copyright © 2024 Daryl Kellie

Edited by Joseph Alexander & Tim Pettingale

www.fundamental-changes.com

For over 350 free guitar lessons with videos check out.

www.fundamental-changes.com

Join our free Facebook Community of Cool Musicians

www.facebook.com/groups/fundamentalguitar

Tag us for a share on Instagram. **FundamentalChanges**

Cover Image Copyright. Shutterstock, Alexander Plonsky

Contents

Introduction

Welcome to an exploration of the rich and enchanting world of Tango guitar. Tango emerged in the late 19th century in the vibrant cities of Buenos Aires and Montevideo, and was born from a melting pot of cultures. Blending African rhythms, European melodies and local flavours, it evolved into a unique and expressive art form. Originally, it was the soundtrack of the dance halls and brothels, where the bandoneón, violin and piano combined to create the iconic sound we recognise today.

The early days of Tango, known as the Guardia Vieja (Old Guard) era spanned from 1880 to 1920 and were characterised by lively, rhythmic tunes and simple harmonies. As the music transitioned into the Guardia Nueva (New Guard) between 1920 and 1955, it became more sophisticated as it began to add elements of jazz and classical music. The mid-20th century witnessed another revolution, brought about by Astor Piazzolla's innovative style of Nuevo Tango, which introduced Tango to audiences around the world.

The guitar has been central to this musical evolution and has always held a special place in Tango's unique sound. Initially used to accompany singers and dancers, the guitar quickly adapted to Tango's ever-changing styles. It provides the harmonic foundation and rhythmic drive essential to the music in ensembles, yet truly shines in solo situations as it showcases the rich melodies and complex harmonies that make Tango so captivating.

This book is inspired by the following three influential guitarists who have shaped the world of Tango by blending tradition with innovation:

Roberto Grela. His collaborations with Aníbal Troilo set new standards for Tango guitar. Grela's intricate arrangements and melodic sensibility brought a depth to Tango music that continues to inspire musicians today.

Aníbal Arias. Renowned for his impeccable technique and expressive playing, Arias' influence resonates in the performances of countless musicians who have followed in his footsteps.

Hugo Rivas. A contemporary master celebrated for his virtuosic playing and profound understanding of traditional Tango. Rivas captures the essence of Tango with a technical brilliance and emotional intensity that is nothing short of mesmerizing.

These guitarists have not only enriched the genre but have also inspired new generations to explore this vibrant musical tradition. As we delve into their dazzling styles and the magic of Tango guitar, they should be at the front of your listening list to help you absorb the heart and soul of the music.

Daryl Kellie

November 2024

Get the Audio

The audio files for this book are available to download for free from **www.fundamental-changes.com.** The link is in the top right-hand corner. Click on the Guitar link then simply select this book title from the drop-down menu and follow the instructions to get the audio.

We recommend that you download the files directly to your computer, not to your tablet, and extract them there before adding them to your media library. You can then put them onto your tablet, iPod or burn them to CD. On the download page there are instructions, and we also provide technical support via the contact form.

For over 350 free guitar lessons with videos check out.

www.fundamental-changes.com

Join our free Facebook Community of Cool Musicians

www.facebook.com/groups/fundamentalguitar

Tag us for a share on Instagram. **FundamentalChanges**

Chapter One: Chord Voicings and Substitutions

This chapter might come across as a little theory-heavy, but you don't need to understand everything when it comes to how we form the important Tango chord progressions below. Just learn the chord sequences and voicings, and don't worry about the theory – it's just as valid to learn all this just by sound. In fact, that's the most common way to learn music.

To begin our exploration of Tango guitar techniques, let's start with some chord voicings that you may already be familiar with, arranged in a simple *marcato* rhythm. Use a pick to strum each chord, and slightly mute the strings after each strike to achieve a crisp staccato effect. This approach will help you to capture the sharp, rhythmic pulse that is essential to Tango music.

Example 1a

Starting from these simple chords, we can expand our harmonic palette by adding inversions and using back cycling and tritone substitutions. These techniques will immediately add some variety and complexity to your playing, allowing you to delve deeper into the rich harmonic textures that define Tango music. Let's look at these ideas in turn.

Inversions

Inversions are alternative ways of playing a chord by changing the order in which the notes are stacked.

For example, the C Major chord contains the notes C, E and G. If we put a note other than C in the bass, we have created an inversion.

Root position = C, E, G

First inversion = E, G, C

Second inversion = G, C, E

If we were to create a CMaj7 chord by adding the 7th (B) to that major triad, we could then create a third inversion chord voicing with the 7th as the lowest note.

Let's play inversions of a C7 chord, which has the notes C, E, G, Bb. This is a useful way of changing the root note position. As you strum, be careful to mute any unwanted notes on the fifth string.

Example 1b

Now try this pattern that changes inversion through an Am chord. Notice in this example, that we create an unusual voicing by playing the 6th (F#) as the root.

Example 1c

Next, here is the chord progression from Example 1a but with changes of inversion. These create smoother transitions between the chords and add harmonic interest to your playing. Practice strumming each chord with a *marcato* rhythm, use a pick and mute slightly after each strike to create a staccato effect.

Example 1d

Back Cycling

Back cycling is the process of moving through a series of chords that lead to a target chord, to create smoother, more interesting transitions. If we take a simple chord change like G major to C major, for example, we can insert chords that enhance the harmonic progression instead of moving directly between them.

Example 1e

We can spice up this progression by adding a ii–V–I progression leading into C major. In the key of C Major, the ii chord is Dm7, the V chord is G7, and the I chord is C major. Adding these chords creates a smooth, satisfying resolution to the C major chord.

Inserting the Dm7 before the G7 creates a stronger harmonic pull towards the C major chord and makes the whole transition more engaging.

Example 1f

To develop this idea further, we can add secondary dominants into the chord sequence. I.e., make both the ii and V chords a dominant 7, so that we have:

D7 – G7 – C

The original dominant chord in the progression was G7. By changing Dm7 to D7, we've now added the dominant chord of G7 – known as a *secondary dominant*.

To develop this progression further we can back cycle further. We could, for example, add in the ii chord of the secondary dominant we've created, so that our progression becomes:

Am – D7 – G7 – C

Or, if we wanted, we could play the Am chord as A7, so that we have:

A7 – D7 – G7 – C

The latter creates a different sound that really pulls us out of the key before it resolves to the C major chord.

We can apply this concept to minor keys too. In Example 1g we are adding a minor ii–V–i sequence in the key of D Minor into the progression, with Em7b5 and A7#5 chords creating a temporary tonal pull towards the D minor chord.

Example 1g

Tri-Tone Substitutions

Tri-tone substitution replaces a dominant chord with another dominant chord a tri-tone (a b5 interval or three whole tones) away.

For example, instead of resolving back to C major, like this sequence…

Example 1h

…we could replace the G7 chord with a Db7 (or in this case Db7b5), which is a tri-tone away from G7, and then resolve to C major:

Example 1i

Another way of adding fluidity to this progression is to use diminished chords as "connecting chords". Diminished chords want to resolve to another chord in the same way as dominant 7s, and can be used to create smooth, chromatic transitions between chords, as in Example 1j.

Example 1j

We've explored several ways in which we can enhance an otherwise routine chord progression – all of which are common approaches to Tango guitar harmony. Now, let's explore these ideas more musically in a Tango chord study that incorporates most of the concepts.

It begins with pianistic chord embellishments. While these are simple to play on the piano, they require large fretting hand stretches on the guitar. To manage these stretches effectively, keep your thumb well behind the neck, practice slowly at first, and gradually work them up to speed.

Example 1k

In the study piece, there are some common syncopated Tango rhythm patterns. We will explore these more thoroughly in the next chapter, but for now this is one of the most important patterns you should know. Notice how it emphasises the "&" of beat 1 and the downbeat of beat 3.

Example 1l

You'll see a few arpeggiated parts in the study below. A useful one to know occurs when a D minor is embellished by lowering the root note to the major 7th (C#), then to the b7th (C), and finally to the 6th (B). This is a great technique to get more mileage out of an otherwise unexciting minor chord.

Example 1m

Now, let's bring together all the techniques we've explored so far – chord inversions, back cycling, tritone substitutions, secondary dominants, minor ii–V–i progressions, chord embellishments, and arpeggiated passages – into a comprehensive study piece.

It's always important to apply concepts in a real-world musical context, and to understand through practical playing how the techniques combine to create the rich, expressive harmonies that define Tango guitar.

Example 1n

F7 F/A E/G♯ E7/B Am E7 Am C♯dim7
Dm G7(♭9) Cmaj7 C6
let ring
B∅ B♭9(♯11) Am7 D/A Am7 D/A A7(♭9)
<5>
Dmadd9 Dm(maj7)add9 Dm/C Ddim/B Cmaj7 G/A Cmaj7 C6
let ring
B∅ E/G♯
1.
Am E/G♯ Am/E C♯dim
2.
Am E(♭13) Am

Chapter Two: Tango Rhythm Guitar

In the previous chapter, we looked at some chord sequences which we played primarily using *marcato* strumming – a technique built around strong, accented downstrokes on the beat. This approach emphasises the rhythm and drives the music forward, capturing the energetic essence of Tango.

Now, let's explore some of the other rhythmic ideas available to us in the Tango style.

The first is a simple but effective way to add interest and tension to a chord pattern by sliding into chords from below. This glissando effect is known as the "Tango drag" or *el arrastre*. Don't worry too much about where you start the slide – it should be fairly undefined, leading up to a distinct destination chord.

Example 2a

To put this technique into musical context, we'll add a full bar of *marcato* voicing changes after the slide, as we learned in Chapter One.

Example 2b

Next, hear how this technique can be applied with smaller rhythmic divisions to add a real bounce to the music.

Example 2c

Here's a dotted rhythm you can try. Notice how the voicing changes are similar to the ideas in Chapter One, but the shift in rhythm completely transforms the musical landscape.

Example 2d

Let's extend this concept by adding a melodic tail at the end.

Example 2e

Síncopa (syncopation) is created by placing rhythmic accents on off-beats or weaker beats, creating a sense of tension and release.

Below is a classic Tango *síncopa*.

Example 2f

Another distinctive Tango rhythm is known as *La Yumba* and was popularised by Osvaldo Pugliese. It features heavy accents on the first and third beats of a 4/4 measure. The name is an onomatopoeic description of the rhythm itself.

Although originally a piano technique, we can imitate the sound of the low piano note clusters on beats 2 and 4 by playing quiet open strings on the guitar.

Example 2g

To make the pitch less distinct (which is useful when playing in keys where the open strings clash) quickly mute the strings on beats 2 and 4.

Example 2h

The final rhythmic device we'll explore in this chapter is the 3-3-2 pattern. This is named for how the 1/8th notes (quavers) in a bar of 4/4 are divided into two groups of three, and one group of two.

1 2 3, 1 2 3, 1 2

This creates accents on beat 1, the "&" of beat 2, and on beat 4. A typical riff or bassline using these accents might look like this.

Example 2i

We can expand on this by outlining the chords, either with arpeggios…

Example 2j

…or by playing the chords themselves.

Example 2k

Now, let's combine some of the ideas explored in this chapter into another rhythmic study piece.

After playing a few variations of the riff shown in Example 2d, you'll tackle some fast, broken chord passages that link into the melodic lines on the high strings. For these sections, use alternate picking and hold the chord shapes (Fm and G7b9) for the full duration (indicated by the *let ring* direction).

Example 2l

Next is a variation of the 3-3-2 pattern that uses 1/16th notes instead of 1/8th notes. The first two bars include A minor and E major chord shapes, featuring a recurring F natural note on the 3rd fret. The next two bars expand the idea with a harmonic minor scale melody on the low strings.

Example 2m

When you feel confident with these exercises, try playing the full study piece which integrates the rhythmic devices and techniques we've discussed. Listen to the audio recording first, then focus on capturing the dynamics of the piece and play as expressively as you can.

Example 2n

E7 Am E7 Am6
Da Coda 1. 2.
E7 Am F7 E/G♯ Am F7 E/G♯ Am
G7 G/B G/D G7 G/B G/D C C/E C/G C C/E C/G
G7 G/B G/D G7 G/B G/D C C/E C/G C C/E C/G
Fm C6add9 A7(♯5) G7(♭9) E7
let ring
let ring
TAB

let ring
let ring
D.S. al Coda
Fm
C6add9
A7(♯5)
G7(♭9)
F7
E/G♯
Am
let ring
let ring

Chapter Three: Further Rhythmic and Stylistic Playing

We've spent the last two chapters learning how to create some vibrant guitar accompaniments. Through the examples and etudes, you'll have begun to build a solid rhythmic foundation that will serve you well across much of the genre. However, there are two other important rhythms and dances you need to know: the Waltz (*Vals*) and the *Milonga*.

The Waltz (*Vals*) is a dance in 3/4 time. On the guitar, we often accompany the dancers by playing a low note or part of the chord on beat 1, and the higher parts of the chord voicing on beats 2 and 3, all with down strums of the pick.

Example 3a

There are many possible variations available to us. Here is one that uses syncopation to help drive the rhythm along.

Example 3b

This can also be played with a swing feel, reminiscent of a jazz waltz.

Example 3c

Adding occasional melodic embellishments can greatly enhance a waltz. In the low register, you might connect the bass notes (*bordoneos*).

Example 3d

In the high register, you can add fills (*rellenos*) to complement the melody.

Example 3e

Try coming up with a few *rellenos* and *bordoneos* of your own to personalise your accompaniment.

The *Milonga* is the final rhythm and dance we'll explore in this chapter. It is characterised by a dotted rhythm at the start of the bar, followed by two even 1/8th notes, and is often notated in 2/4 time.

Example 3f

Try playing this rhythm using a D minor chord.

Example 3g

To tighten up the rhythm, add a slight mute immediately after the first and third strums.

Example 3h

Here is a variation using the *arrastre* technique to slide into the first beat.

Example 3i

You could also add a *milonga* bass riff that outlines the arpeggios.

Example 3j

Next, here's a variation on the 3-3-2 rhythm in the key of D Minor. Here, you can see how the open strings are useful in helping to make this kind of riff resonate.

Try coming up with some of your own variations in other keys.

Example 3k

As the piece below builds in intensity, a unison part is played between the bandoneón and the guitar. This kind of idea is a great way to create drama and tension in Tango, as it breaks away from the usual chordal texture and eventually resolves with an idiosyncratic V–I ending.

Example 3l

Let's look at a short *Milonga* study to combine some of these elements together musically. You will recognise many of the ideas from earlier in the chapter.

Once you are confident with these techniques, try playing the full study along with the audio track. This will help you internalise the rhythms and embellishments we've discussed and deepen your understanding of how they are used to create drama and tension in Tango music.

Example 3m

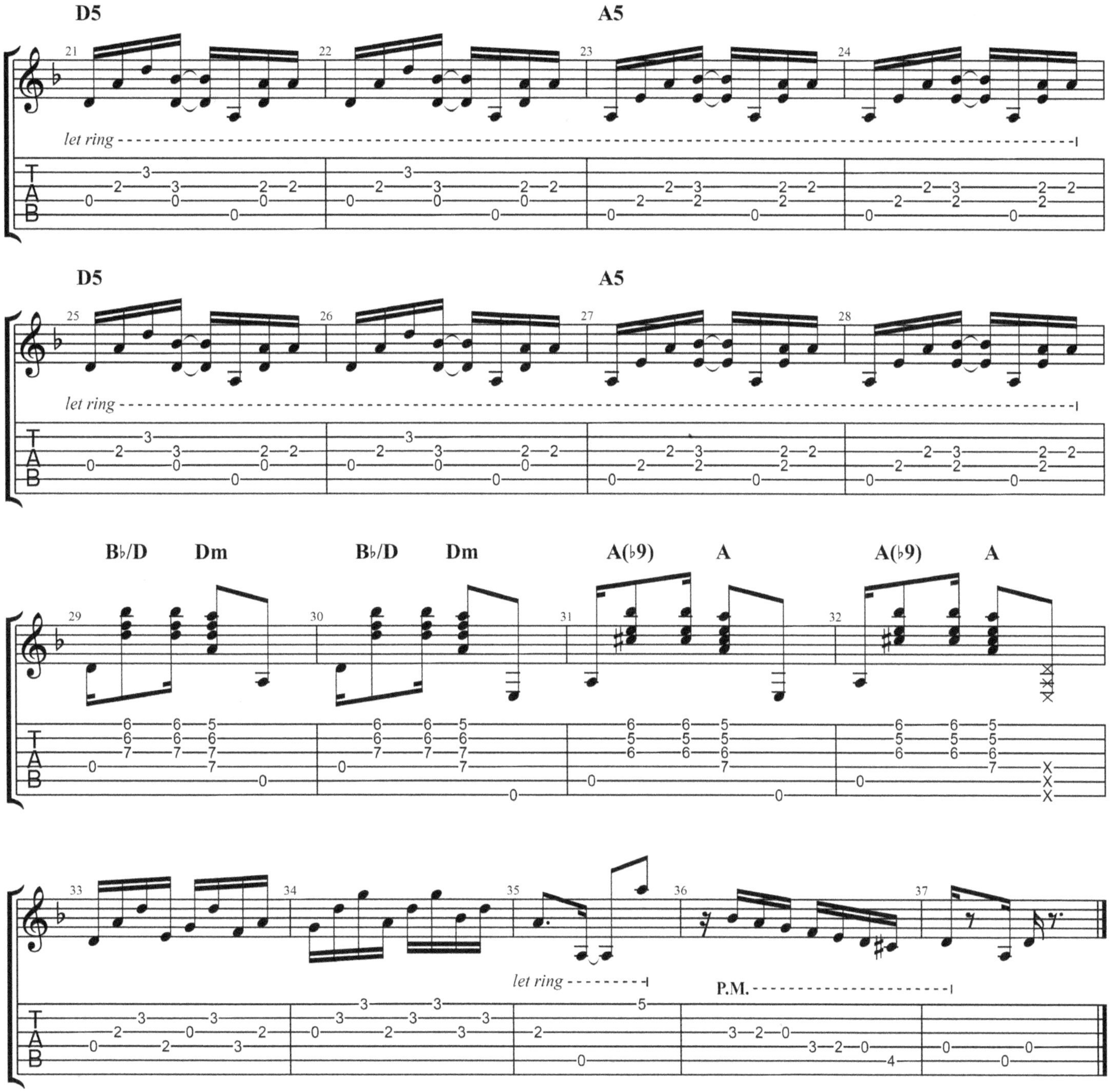
D5
A5
let ring
D5
A5
let ring
B♭/D
Dm
B♭/D
Dm
A(♭9)
A
A(♭9)
A
let ring
P.M.

Chapter Four: Melodic Improvisation in Tango

Tango is a genre steeped in passion, emotion, and intricate melodic lines. When improvising in this style, the goal is to blend technical proficiency with expressive phrasing, capturing the essence of Tango in every note.

Previously, we touched on two types of improvised Tango licks: *rellenos* (high-register embellishments that enhance the melody) and *bordoneos* (low-register phrases that connect root notes or basslines). To help you create and develop your own improvisations, let's explore some more essential tools.

The Major Scale

The major scale is foundational in Western music. It is structured using the following intervals:

Whole Step – Whole Step – Half Step – Whole Step – Whole Step – Whole Step – Half Step

In C Major that pattern results in the notes:

C – D – E – F – G – A – B – C

Here is a useful major shape you should know, using the C Major scale.

Example 4a

Now, let's work with a melody in C Major based around that shape.

Example 4b

To create depth, let's add a simple ascending line from the same scale to complement the melody.

Example 4c

Alternatively, a descending line might create a different feeling.

Example 4d

To make the phrase more expressive, try adding a slide into one of the notes. This subtle technique can bring life and personality to your playing.

Example 4e

Minor Scales

Tango frequently uses both the harmonic and melodic minor scales to convey a more dramatic and emotive sound.

The Harmonic Minor Scale

The Harmonic Minor scale formula is:

Whole Step – Half Step –Whole Step – Whole Step – Half Step – Whole-and-a-Half Step – Half Step

Those intervals produce the following notes in the A Harmonic Minor scale:

A – B – C – D – E – F – G# – A

The raised 7th (G#) note especially brings the tension and atmosphere typical of Tango.

Example 4f

Here's a melody using the A Harmonic Minor scale in the same register.

Example 4g

To embellish this melody, you might add a flourish leading into the G#.

Use your third finger to perform a hammer-on and pull-off, then slide your first finger down to the G# on the 4th fret to add some sophisticated flair to your playing.

Example 4h

You can also apply a similar idea at the end of the phrase to finish with a flourish.

Example 4i

The Melodic Minor Scale

The melodic minor scale is another powerful tool in Tango improvisation and, unusually, it is played differently in its ascending and descending forms.

For example, the A Melodic Minor scale ascending is:

A – B – C – D – E – F# – G# – A

Notice that it is similar to A Harmonic Minor but has a major 6th (F#) instead of a b6 (F).

Descending, A Melodic Minor is played:

A – G – F – E – D – C – B – A

(The same notes as the A Natural Minor scale).

Example 4j

Here's an example of how you might use the ascending form to decorate the previous melody, creating a tonal pull back up to the tonic (A).

Example 4k

Alternatively, use the descending (natural minor) form in the middle of a phrase to smoothly lead into the D on the 7th fret.

Example 4l

Chromatic Passing Notes

Chromatic (or "non-scale") *passing notes* can be added to melodies to create tension, and the smooth transitions that are characteristic of Tango improvisations. These notes are not part of the scale or chord but are just used to connect diatonic notes (notes within the scale) in a melodic line.

How to Use Chromatic Passing Notes

1. Between Scale Degrees

You can add a chromatic note between two scale notes to create a fluid, connected sound that adds some tension to your melody. For example, in a C Major scale, you could play a C# note (normally on a weak beat of the bar) to connect the notes C and D.

Example 4m

2. Approaching Chord Tones

You can also add chromatic notes to approach the tones of the chord you are soloing over to create a sense of pull and anticipation.

Example 4n

Tango Phrasing

In Tango, chromaticism is often used to add dramatic flair. We can experiment by adding chromatic runs that resolve to a chord tone to intensify the emotional impact of our lines.

Example 4o

Exercises

To internalise these concepts, try the following exercises.

Play this melody in the key of A Minor.

Example 4p

Rhythmic Variations

Next, choose some chromatic notes to add between the 2nd (B) and 6th (F) degrees to create a more intricate line. Now play the melody with various rhythmic patterns to understand how the chromatic notes impact the feel.

Example 4q

Example 4r

Example 4s

Practice with Backing Track

Learn this melody and play along with the backing track provided for this example.

Example 4t

Next, in the indicated places, improvise a short phrase using one or more of the tools we've discussed, or choose your favourite techniques. Here are some examples to help you get started.

Example 4u

Have Fun Exploring

Remember, the key to mastering Tango improvisation lies in combining technical skill with expressive, heartfelt playing. As you explore these scales and techniques, focus on how they can convey emotion and tell a musical story.

Let your creativity flow, and don't be afraid to experiment with different ideas. The beauty of Tango lies in its ability to capture deep emotions, so immerse yourself in the music and enjoy the journey of becoming a more expressive guitarist. Don't forget to listen to as much Tango as you can to help inspire your exploration.

Chapter Five: Further Melodic Improvisation

In the previous chapter we started to explore melodic improvisation in Tango music. Now we will look in greater detail at why we choose certain notes at certain points in the music. Much of this decision is based around which chord is being played at the time.

Identifying "Safe" Notes

Understanding which notes sound consonant (at rest) over particular chords is essential for effective improvisation. These notes are often the chord tones and guide tones within the harmony.

Chord Tones

The root, 3rd and 5th of a chord are typically the strongest, most stable notes to land on during improvisation, and provide a solid foundation for your melody. In C Major, these notes are:

C (root), **E** (3rd) and **G** (5th).

When you are improvising with the C Major scale, here is how to find those notes.

Example 5a

By targeting these chord tones in your solos, often on strong beats, you create melodies that sound well-integrated with the underlying harmony.

Guide Tones

The 3rd and 7th intervals of a chord (for example, the notes E and B that belong to a CMaj7) play an important role in defining its harmonic quality.

They are useful to target in your melody, especially during chord transitions, as they can smoothly lead the listener from one harmonic space to another.

For instance, when moving from G7 to a C major:

In G7, the 7th is F.

In C major, the 3rd is E.

By playing a melody line that moves from the F (7th of G7) to the E (3rd of C major) you beautifully outline the chord change.

Example 5b

Similarly, on an E7 to Am chord change:

In E7 the 7th is D.

In Am the 3rd is C.

A phrase that moves from D to C highlights the transition between these chords.

Example 5c

Arpeggios

Arpeggios are useful tools in improvisation because they contain all of a chord's notes, allowing you to outline the harmony clearly while playing a melodic line. By breaking down chords into their individual notes, you can navigate a chord sequence very effectively.

Learn this useful arpeggio shape for C major and think about how it relates to the chord.

Example 5d

Here's a similar arpeggio shape for A minor.

Example 5e

While only playing chord tones ensures your notes fit "safely" within the harmony, it can also make your playing sound predictable and lacking in interest. To add depth and colour to your solos, it's important to add other scale and chromatic notes.

Mixing Scales with Arpeggios

To create more dynamic and engaging solos we can blend scale passages with arpeggios to introduce both linear (scale-based) and vertical (arpeggio-based) elements into your improvisation.

For example, over an E7 chord that moves to Am, you can mix notes from the E7 arpeggio (E, G#, B, D) with scale lines from the A Harmonic Minor scale, eventually resolving to the b3 of the A minor chord (C).

Example 5f

Similarly, over a G7 to C major chord change, you could use a chromatic line to add tension before resolving to the 3rd (E) of the C major chord.

Example 5g

The Importance of "Safe" Notes

Identifying and targeting safe notes – those that sound consonant and resolve well over chord changes – is a crucial skill in improvisation. It enhances the musicality of your solos and ensures that your improvisations complement the underlying harmony.

Practical Exercises

Let's put these concepts into practice by soloing over a simple chord progression using Am, Dm and E7 chords. Focus on targeting the chord tones, especially the 3rd and 7th of each chord, and observe how they resolve within the progression.

Exercise 1. Scale-Based Solo

Using the notes of the A Harmonic Minor scale, improvise over the backing track. Concentrate on your phrasing and rhythm to create expressive melodies.

Here are some ideas to get you started.

Example 5h

Exercise 2. Arpeggio-Based Solo

Create a solo that primarily utilises arpeggios from the Am, Dm and E7 chords. Mix in passing notes for added flavour and to enhance the melodic flow.

Try experimenting with different arpeggio patterns.

Example 5i

Exercise 3. Chromatic Approach

Add chromatic passing notes to connect chord tones and add tension to your solos. Experiment with different placements of these chromatic notes to evoke various emotional effects.

Here's an example.

Example 5j

Putting It All Together

By combining these approaches, using scale passages, arpeggios, and chromatic embellishments, you can create solos that are both harmonically sound and emotionally engaging. Remember to listen to how each note interacts with the chords and strive for melodic lines that tell a story.

I have included audio examples of these solos to guide you, but be sure to use the backing track to try out your own ideas. Don't hesitate to mix and match the techniques we've discussed to discover what most resonates with you.

Ear Training Tips

Developing a keen ear is essential for recognising and using these important notes. Here are some practices to help strengthen your ear and improvisational skills.

- **Sing the Notes.** Sing along with your scales, arpeggios and solos. This strengthens the connection between what you hear and what you play, improving your ability to internalise melodies

- **Transcribe Solos.** Listen to Tango solos by master musicians and transcribe them. Analyse which notes are being targeted over each chord and how they contribute to the overall expression

- **Play by Ear.** Practice playing simple melodies by ear, gradually progressing to more complex lines. This helps you to internalise the sound of the "good notes" and how they function over different chords

Chapter Six: Tango Chord Melody

Chord melody is a sophisticated, expressive style of playing where we simultaneously perform both the melody *and* the accompanying chords of a piece. This allows a solo guitarist to blend harmony and melody in a richer way that mimics the depth of a full band.

By mastering some basic chord melody techniques, you can perform complete arrangements of songs without needing other instruments to accompany you.

To show you the process, we're going to create a simple chord melody arrangement of the Tango classic *El Choclo*.

First, familiarise yourself with the main melody of *El Choclo*.

Example 6a

Learning the melody on its own is crucial. Pay attention to the phrasing and its nuances to capture the essence of the Tango style. This melody is the foundation upon which we'll build the entire chord melody arrangement.

The first chord in the tune is Dm. A simple way to introduce this harmony is to add the root note and any parts of the chord available to use between the pitch of the melody note and the root.

Use a pick to strum through these voicings in the style of Hugo Rivas.

Example 6b

While this approach provides a basic accompaniment, it lacks some of the interest and movement characteristic of Tango harmony. It's a good starting point, but there's room for improvement.

To enrich the arrangement, let's add some of the ideas we studied in Chapter One. We'll begin by changing inversions of the Dm chord. By altering the chord inversions, we create smoother voice-leading and a more engaging harmonic progression.

Additionally, we create a motif with the open A and D strings, which we'll develop later in the arrangement.

Example 6c

Next, let's add a descending chromatic line leading down to the A chord. The open string bass-note motif is referenced again, this time using the open E and A strings to outline the A7 chord. The descending chromatic line adds tension and guides the listener smoothly into the chord change to improve the flow of the piece.

Example 6d

Example 6e extends this idea over the next few bars. I've added a slide and pull-off to the open D string, creating a unison between the melody and bass note on neighbouring strings.

Example 6e

These articulations (slides and pull-offs) not only create more nuanced phrasing, they also add to the expressive quality of the music.

As we lead into the Gm chord , notice how the various voicings of the D7 chord create a strong tonal pull towards the new key. The open string motif is referenced once more, but this time using natural harmonics on the 5th fret. Using natural harmonics introduces a shimmering texture to highlight the transition and adds some sophistication to the arrangement.

Example 6f

The main melody concludes with a descending line played under a Gm chord that leads back into the Dm. This is followed by some parallel 3rds and a final I–V–I resolution.

Example 6g

In the next section we change the rhythm of the accompanying chords. By placing them on off-beats and varying their placement there's less to play, but this still provides a driving and compelling rhythmic backdrop – a useful approach to chord melody arrangement.

Example 6h

In the final section, we add numerous embellishments and some more advanced techniques. Use alternating pick strokes for the fast melodic lines to maintain clarity and speed, and ensure that the harmonics ring clearly.

For the strummed harmonics, lay your fretting finger lightly across the node point on the fret and lift it immediately after the strum to allow the harmonics to ring and sustain.

Example 6i

Now, let's put the entire arrangement of *El Choclo* together.

Example 6j

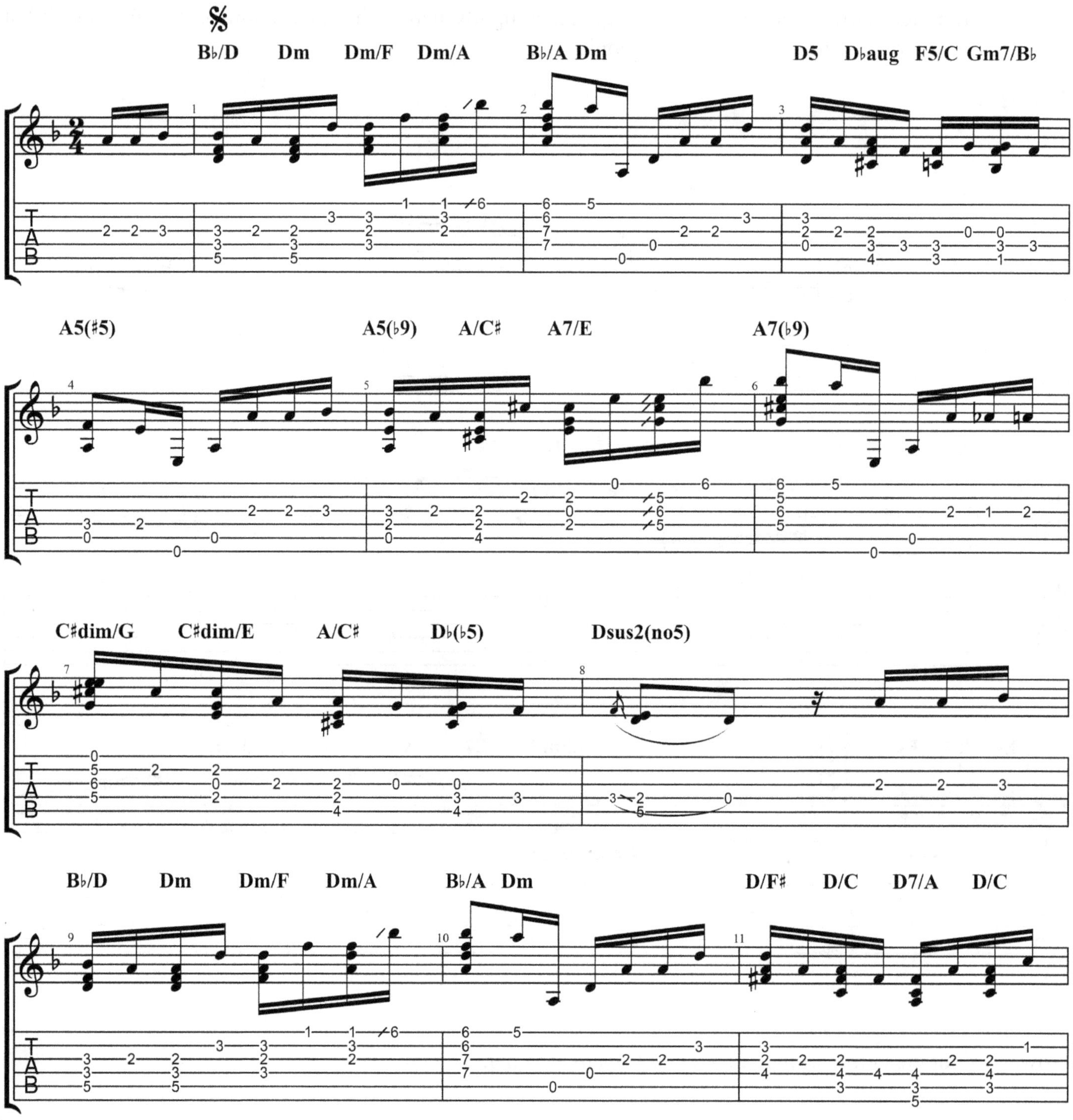
B♭/D Dm Dm/F Dm/A B♭/A Dm D5 D♭aug F5/C Gm7/B♭
A5(♯5) A5(♭9) A/C♯ A7/E A7(♭9)
C♯dim/G C♯dim/E A/C♯ D♭(♭5) Dsus2(no5)
B♭/D Dm Dm/F Dm/A B♭/A Dm D/F♯ D/C D7/A D/C
TAB
TAB
TAB
TAB

Gmadd11
Gm6 B♭maj7/F Gm/E B♭/D
Dsus2/F
let ring
fine
Asus4/E
Dm/F A7 D5/A
C7/G
Fsus4 Fmaj7
Gm7 C7
F6(no5)
let ring
A7/E
Dsus4 Dm
E/G♯
let ring
1.
2.
A7
A/G
D/F♯

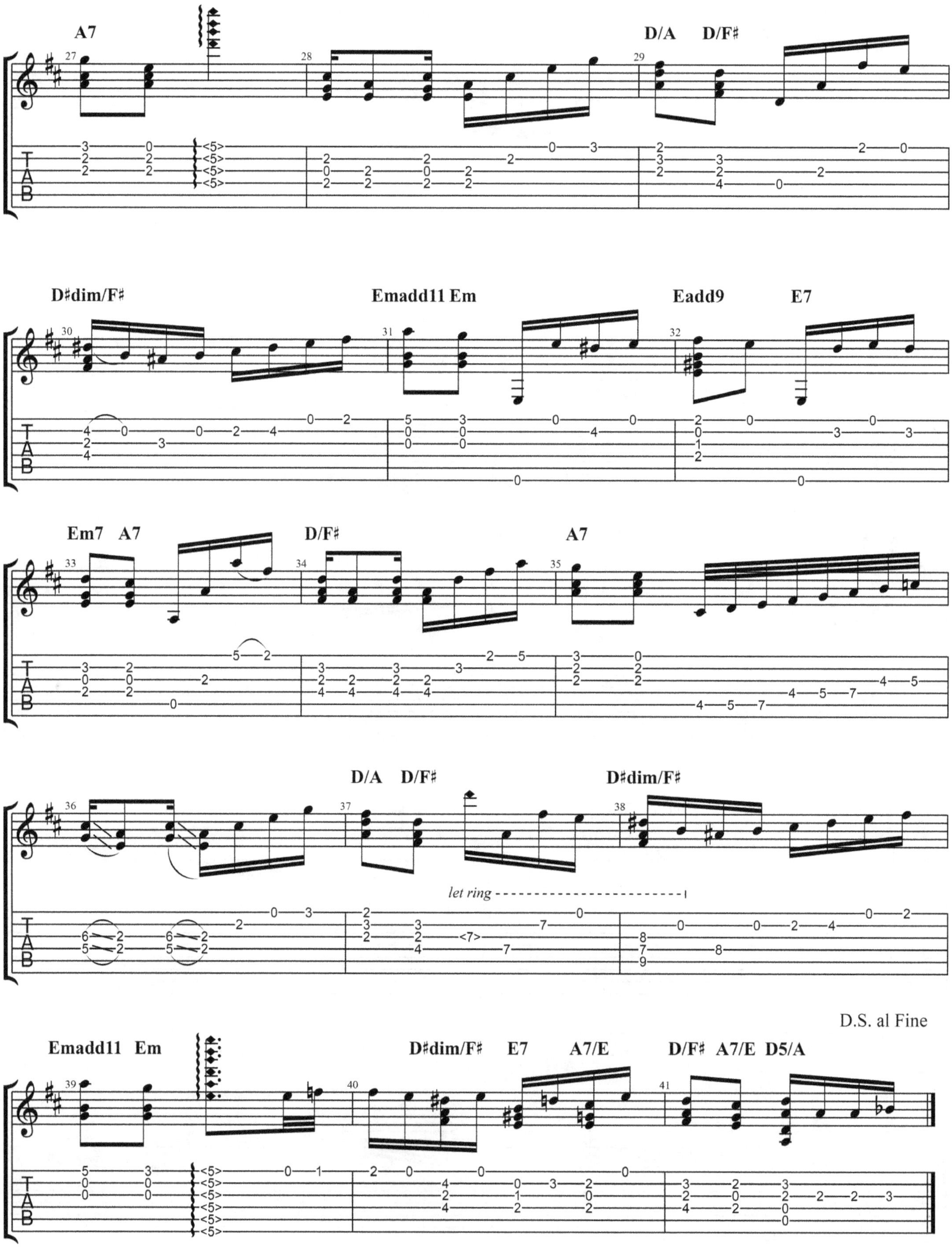
A7
D/A D/F♯
D♯dim/F♯
Emadd11 Em
Eadd9 E7
Em7 A7
D/F♯
A7
D/A D/F♯
D♯dim/F♯
let ring
D.S. al Fine
Emadd11 Em
D♯dim/F♯ E7 A7/E
D/F♯ A7/E D5/A

By combining all the techniques and ideas we've explored in this chapter we can create a rich, engaging chord melody arrangement that captures the spirit of Tango.

As you work through this arrangement, follow these tips:

- **Practice Slowly.** Take your time with each section, ensuring that you understand how each technique contributes to the overall sound

- **Focus on Expression.** Pay attention to dynamics and phrasing to bring out the emotional depth of the music

- **Refine Your Technique.** Work on clean execution of slides, pull-offs, harmonics, and rhythmic variations

By dedicating time to these aspects, you'll enhance not only your technical skills but also your musicality.

Don't hesitate to experiment with your own ideas. Try applying these techniques to other pieces or when composing your own chord melody arrangements. The more you explore, the more you'll develop your voice on the guitar.

Chapter Seven: Counterpoint and More

In this chapter we will expand upon the chord melody approach by adding *counterpoint* – the playing of multiple melodies on different strings that move both independently and harmoniously.

The guitar allows us to play intertwining melodies that add texture and depth to our music. Though counterpoint is often associated with classical music from the Baroque period, it is often used beautifully in Tango.

Counterpoint enriches your playing by creating independent melodic voices, where each melody line has its own contour and rhythm. This has the effect of adding richness and complexity while evoking a wide range of emotions.

Let's begin with a simple melody in A Major. This melody will serve as the foundation for our exploration of counterpoint.

Example 7a

One easy way to enrich this melody is to underpin it with a ii–V–I progression. This adds harmonic support but doesn't fully utilise counterpoint, as the harmony moves in block chords rather than as independent lines.

Example 7b

Now we have added more chords, we can compose another melody to complement the original one. By choosing notes that hint at the V–I harmony from the previous example, we might create something like this. Notice that this second line has its own melodic integrity and would stand alone as a melody in its own right.

Example 7c

Now, the two melodies move in *contrary motion* – one ascends while the other descends – yet they eventually become unison for a satisfying resolution. Use your fingers for the higher-register notes and your thumb for the lower ones as this will allow you to articulate each voice clearly.

Example 7d

Here's another example with the two voices moving in opposite directions. The combination of both chromatic and diatonic lines is a common characteristic of Tango.

Notice that the higher voice finishes on A (the root note of A major) and the lower voice finishes on C# (the 3rd of A major). These two thicken the sound of this chord and accentuate the harmony. This interplay between voices adds depth and a sense of conversation within the music.

Example 7e

Let's consider another melody, this time resolving to D major.

Example 7f

To add depth, let's add a low descending melody that complements the initial line. Notice that there's plenty of space to add other notes between the two melodies. By moving some notes to different strings we avoid tricky fingering stretches and ensure that the counterpoint is playable and can flow smoothly.

Example 7g

Next, I add notes to form a fuller G/B chord.

The Gm9/Bb chord occurs naturally by allowing the melody notes to sustain.

The final two bars use a descending melody on the G string to create a three-part counterpoint. The descending line moves from the 7th fret, down via B and Bb to A, the 5th of the D major chord for a satisfying conclusion.

Example 7h

Counterpoint in *Don Juan* by Ernesto Ponzio

Now, let's put these ideas into practice with an arrangement of one of the oldest Tango melodies, *Don Juan* by Ernesto Ponzio.

Begin with your thumb playing the *Milonga* riff on the low strings while slightly palm muting. This creates a rhythmic foundation and captures an authentic Tango feel. Release the palm mute as the melody enters. Use your index and middle fingers to pick the melody, and the harmonised notes in 3rds, while your thumb continues to pick the bass riff.

Example 7i

In the piece below you'll also notice occasional harmonics embellishing the melody, indicated by diamond-shaped notes. To play these harmonics, lightly touch the string directly above the fret wire at the harmonic node (the 7th fret in this case), then pluck the string to produce a bell-like tone as you remove your finger. Precision is key here, so take your time to find the exact spot where the harmonic rings clearly.

Example 7j

When finger picking, coordinating your thumb and fingers is essential. In this arrangement, apart from in the intro riff, any notes with stems pointing down should be picked with the thumb, while notes with stems pointing up should be picked with your fingers. Aim for an even volume between the bass and melody to balance the dynamics the piece.

When working on these complex counterpoint sections, it's essential to practice slowly. Take the time to isolate challenging passages and play them at a reduced tempo. Focus on clarity by ensuring each voice is distinct and the notes are cleanly articulated. As you gain confidence, you can gradually increase the speed until you reach the performance tempo.

Now, here's the full arrangement of *Don Juan*. Take your time learning each section and, most importantly, enjoy the process of exploring the interplay of melodies.

Example 7k

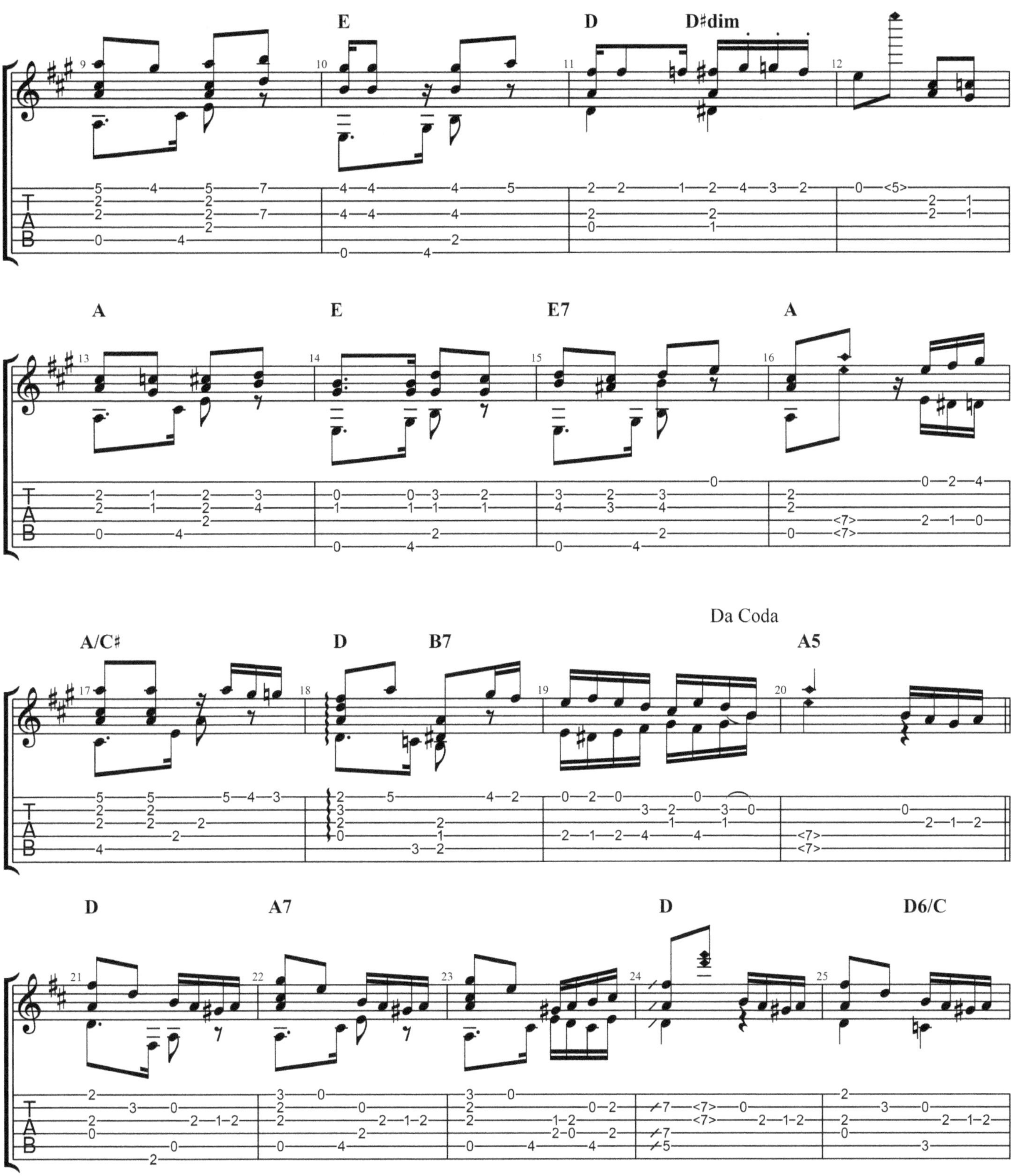
E
D
D♯dim
A
E
E7
A
Da Coda
A/C♯
D
B7
A5
D
A7
D
D6/C

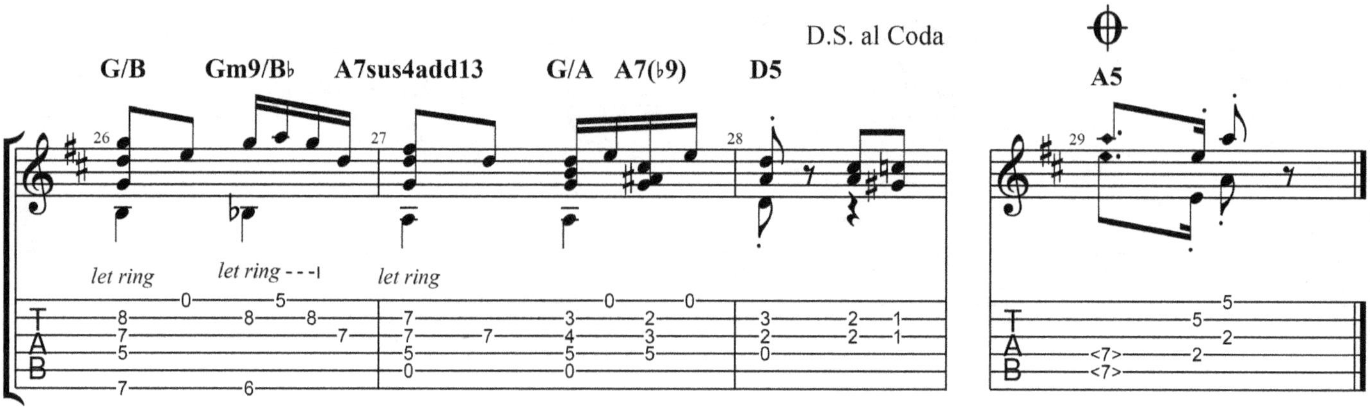
D.S. al Coda
G/B
Gm9/B♭
A7sus4add13
G/A
A7(♭9)
D5
A5
let ring
let ring
let ring
TAB

Chapter Eight: Putting It All Together

Let's bring together everything we've learned by working on an arrangement of the Tango classic *La Cumparsita*. Even if you're not familiar with Tango, the chances are you'll have heard this iconic piece which has been referred to as the Anthem of Tango. Composed by Uruguayan, Gerardo Matos Rodríguez in 1916, it has become synonymous with Tango, embodying both its passion and complexity.

This arrangement is intended as a solo guitar piece to be played with a pick, but many of the chord voicing and substitution techniques can be effectively used in an ensemble setting. The piece consists of three sections (A, B and C), and has an ABACA form, allowing us to revisit themes and apply different techniques to each section.

In the A section, the melody sits above more *marcato* chords that build a strong rhythmic foundation. The melody includes recurring chromatic motifs that add tension and interest. The first *relleno* (an improvised melodic fill) occurs in bar seven.

Notice the intentional dissonance created by the clash of the notes F# and G. This kind of deliberate discord is often referred to as *mugre* (meaning "dirty" in Spanish) and is a beautiful way to add spice and character to your fills.

Example 8a

Into the B section, we will use the descending chromatic line from way back in Example 1m. This type of chromatic idea adds interest and movement to an otherwise static minor chord and is easy to add to your own playing, whether you're comping or crafting a solo arrangement.

Example 8b

In Example 9c, a diminished arpeggio lick is used to outline an A7b9 chord, pulling us back up to the D major chord. The fingering pattern on the fretboard is simple and symmetrical, so repeats every three frets. These notes neatly outline the A7b9 chord by including the intervals:

- C# (3rd)

- E (5th)

- G (b7)

- Bb (b9)

By using this arpeggio, we create a smooth transition back to the D major chord while adding harmonic richness to the arrangement.

Example 8c

We can use the same idea over the E7b9 chord, this time resolving to Am9.

Example 8d

In the second A section, we introduce the 3–3–2 rhythm we studied in Chapter Two.

This rhythm is often used with the b13 motif (here played as Gmb13), but as you can see, it also works well with chord movements like the ii–V–I progression or other interesting substitutions.

Example 8e

Ending a piece with a strong cadence is crucial. Not only does it signal to dancers that the piece is concluding, but it also brings the arrangement to a satisfying close for the audience. The V–I perfect cadence is common in Tango endings, but there are various ways to embellish it with your personal touch.

In the example below, a small pause is used before the final ending to build anticipation and add impact to the final chord. It's also common in Tango for the final I chord to be played much more softly than the V to create a dynamic yet unexpected resolution.

Example 8f

If we replace the V chord with its tritone substitution (for example, substituting Ab7 for D7) we add an unexpected harmonic richness to the ending which can delightfully engage the listener.

Example 8g

Another idea is to approach the V chord chromatically from above. For instance, to play Eb7 then D7 before finally resolving to Gm to add a different tension before the final resolution.

Example 8h

Another option is to add a countermelody as you resolve from V to I to add some richness and complexity to your ending.

Example 8i

It is possible to combine some of these ideas to create musical variations on these endings.

Now that we've explored various techniques and concepts, it's time to apply them to the full arrangement of *La Cumparsita*.

As you work through the piece, remember to:

- **Pay Attention to Dynamics.** Explore the contrast between loud and soft passages to enhance their emotional impact

- **Embrace Dissonance.** Don't shy away from *mugre* moments – they add character to your playing

- **Experiment with Rhythm.** Add different rhythmic patterns to keep the arrangement engaging and fresh

- **Refine Your Ending.** Use the ending techniques discussed above to conclude the piece with confidence and flair

By combining all the elements we've covered throughout this journey – chord voicings, substitutions, rhythmic variations, melodic embellishments, and more – you'll be able to perform *La Cumparsita* as a solo guitar piece that truly captures the essence of Tango.

This arrangement not only serves as a culmination of your learning, it's also the stepping stone to further exploration and creativity in your playing.

Now, here's the full arrangement of *La Cumparsita*. Dive in, enjoy the process, and allow the music to speak through you.

Example 8j

Cmadd9
D/C
D7
G5
Gmadd9
Gm
Gm/F♯
Gm9/F
Cm/E♭
Bdim/D
G7(♯5)
let ring
let ring
let ring
Cm
Gm
D/F♯
A
D
Gm6

D
Gm6
Cmadd9
Cm
Cm(maj7)
Cm
Am7add11
A♭7(♭5)
Gm
Gm(♭13)
Gm
Gm(♭13)
Gm
Adim/C
Cdim/A
D7(♯5)
P.M.
Gm6
C
G5
Gm
G5
Cm
Gm
G5
Gm

G5
Cm
Gm
G7
Cmadd9
Cm/B♭
Cm69
D7sus4/E
D(♭9)/F♯
F♯dim7/A
Am7/D
Gm/D
Csus2/E♭
Cm7/A
Adim/E♭
Edim
D/F♯
Gm
A
D7
TAB

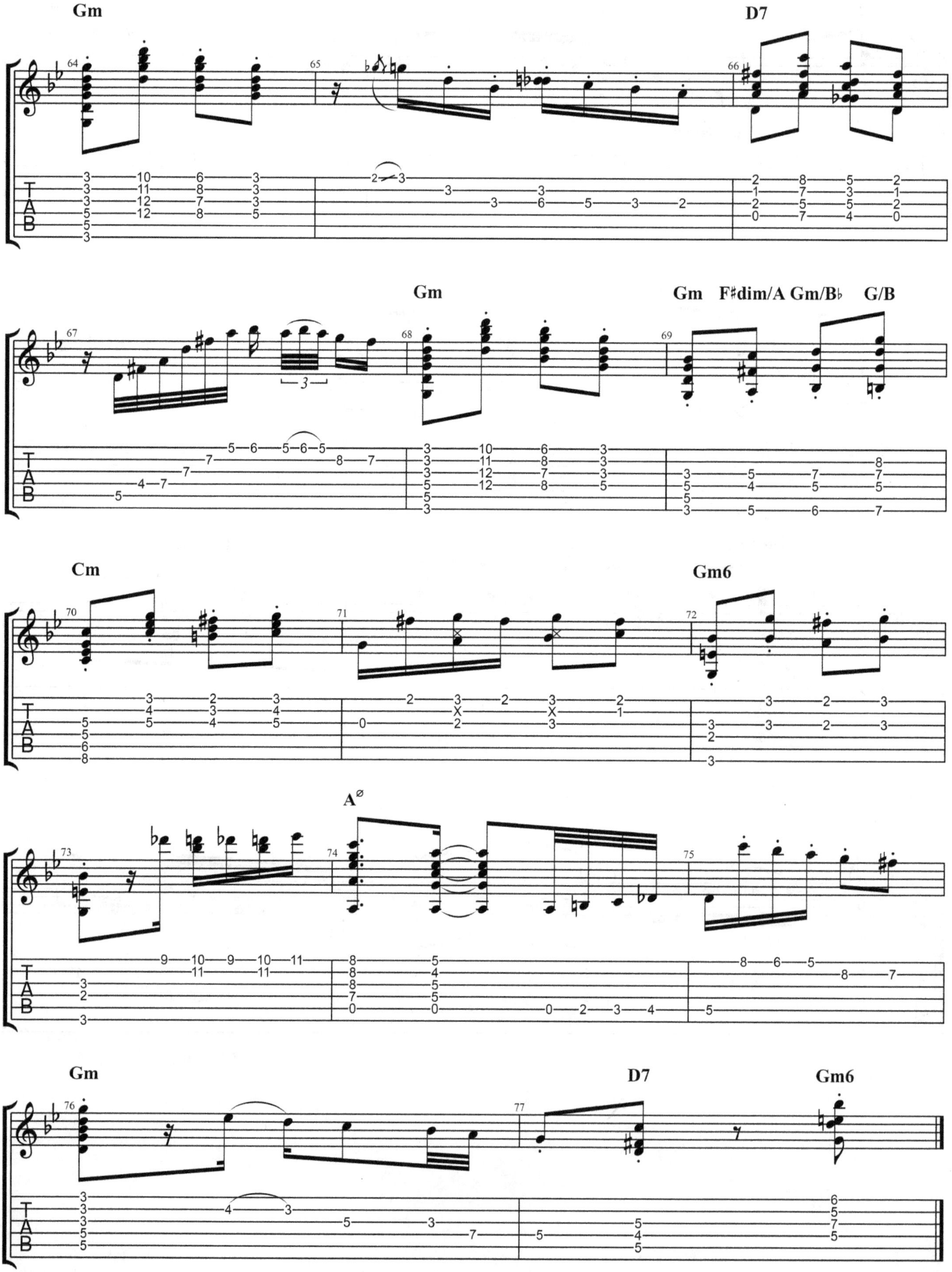
Gm
D7
Gm
Gm F♯dim/A Gm/B♭ G/B
Cm
Gm6
A∅
Gm
D7
Gm6

Chapter Nine: Preparing for the Live Situation

It's essential to have a solid repertoire that resonates with contemporary audiences while maintaining the traditional Tango essence. Here are some key pieces and songs every Tango guitarist should know.

1. *Libertango* by Astor Piazzolla

Why It's Important: This iconic piece represents the evolution of Tango into Nuevo Tango, incorporating elements of jazz and classical music. It's a must-know for its rhythmic complexity and modern Tango feel.

Guitar Tips: Focus on syncopation and dynamic contrasts to capture the piece's intensity.

2. *Oblivion* by Astor Piazzolla

Why It's Important: A deeply emotional and technically challenging piece, it's a cornerstone of Piazzolla's work and a powerful addition to any guitarist's repertoire.

Guitar Tips: Pay close attention to phrasing and the use of *rubato* to convey the piece's emotional depth.

3. *La Cumparsita* by Gerardo Matos Rodríguez

Why It's Important: Often called the Anthem of Tango, this piece is universally recognised and beloved. Knowing how to play it is essential for any Tango guitarist.

Guitar Tips: Master various arrangements, from simple chord-melody to more intricate versions, to adapt to different performance contexts.

4. *El Choclo* by Ángel Villoldo

Why It's Important: One of the most popular Tangos ever composed, *El Choclo* has been interpreted in countless ways. It's a great piece for exploring the interplay between melody and rhythm.

Guitar Tips: Experiment with different strumming patterns and syncopations to make the piece your own.

5. *Milonga del Ángel* by Astor Piazzolla

Why It's Important: This piece showcases a softer, more lyrical side of Tango. It's a beautiful addition to any solo guitar performance.

Guitar Tips: Focus on expressing the lyrical melodies and smooth chord transitions to capture the essence of the *Milonga* rhythm.

6. *Por Una Cabeza* by Carlos Gardel

Why It's Important: A classic Tango song with poignant lyrics, it is a staple in the repertoire of any Tango guitarist who accompanies singers or plays instrumental versions.

Guitar Tips: Pay attention to the harmony and the voice-leading in the chords, as this piece often requires sensitive accompaniment.

7. *Nostalgias* by Juan Carlos Cobián

Why It's Important: Known for its powerful rhythmic drive and intricate arrangements, *Nostalgias* is a challenging but rewarding piece that embodies the orchestral Tango style.

Guitar Tips: Focus on maintaining a strong rhythmic pulse and using accents to bring out the piece's dramatic qualities.

Structure of a Milonga

A *Milonga* (not to be confused with the rhythm of the same name mentioned earlier!) is a social event where people gather to dance Tango. Understanding the structure and flow of a *Milonga* is crucial for any Tango musician, especially if you're performing live. Here's an overview:

Tandas and Cortinas

Music at a *Milonga* is played in sets called *tandas*, usually consisting of 3-4 songs of a similar style. A *tanda* allows dancers to stay with the same partner for a while, fostering a connection through consistent musical themes. Between *tandas*, a short piece of non-Tango music called a *cortina* is played. This signals the end of the *tanda* and provides a break for dancers to change partners.

Types of *Tandas*

Tango Tandas: These are the most common and consist of traditional Tango pieces.

Milonga Tandas: These more rhythmic pieces use the *Milonga (habanera)* type rhythm.

Vals (Waltz) Tandas: Played in 3/4 time, these *tandas* offer a smooth, flowing dance experience.

Nuevo Tandas: These include modern or Nuevo Tango music, often with electronic or jazz influences.

Flow of the Event

The evening usually begins with more traditional, slower Tangos, moving into *Milongas* and *Valses* as the night progresses. As the night goes on, the energy tends to build, with more upbeat and faster *tandas* being played later.

Understanding the Dancers' Needs

Be mindful of the energy on the dance floor. Start with familiar, easy-to-dance-to pieces and gradually introduce more complex rhythms and modern pieces as the night progresses. Also, always end a *tanda* with a strong, recognisable piece to keep the energy high.

Playing *A la Parilla*: Tips for Effective Jamming and Improvisation for Tango Guitarists

Playing *a la parrilla* refers to the practice of improvising or playing without a written arrangement, much like jamming in jazz. Here's how to approach it:

Understand the Form

Familiarise yourself with the standard Tango chord progressions, such as the use of dominant 7th chords, minor keys, and common cadences. Know the basic structures of Tango pieces, such as ABAC or verse-chorus formats and typical introductions and endings.

Develop a Chord Vocabulary

Learn a variety of chord voicings and inversions to create smooth voice leading and to provide harmonic interest. Drop 2 and drop 3 voicings are especially useful here. Practice chord substitutions like tritone subs or passing chords to add richness to your accompaniment.

Rhythmic Variations

Work on mastering *marcato* (strong, accented beats) and syncopation, which are crucial in Tango. Being able to vary your strumming pattern will keep your playing dynamic.

Milonga and Vals Feels. Practice the distinct rhythmic feels of *Milonga* (faster, more percussive) and *Vals* (waltz time) to be able to switch styles fluidly.

Melodic Embellishments

Use typical Tango ornaments such as *bordoneos* and *rellenos* to decorate the melody or harmony while improvising. Engage in musical conversations with other instruments, such as the bandoneón or violin, through call-and-response phrasing.

Listening and Interaction

Pay attention to what other musicians are playing and respond accordingly. In Tango, it's all about interaction and creating a cohesive sound. Make sure you can see and communicate with other musicians using visual prompts (a nod of the head in your direction to gesture that yours is the next solo, for example). Be prepared to adapt your playing to the mood of the moment, whether that means simplifying your playing or stepping up to take a more prominent role.

Accompanying a Singer: Techniques for Supporting Vocal Performances

Accompanying a singer in Tango requires sensitivity and a deep understanding of both the music and the lyrics. Here are some tips:

Understanding the Lyrics

Familiarise yourself with the lyrics of the songs you're accompanying. Tango lyrics often deal with themes of love, loss, and nostalgia, so your playing should reflect the emotional tone of the song. Pay attention to the singer's phrasing and breathe with them. Your playing should support their interpretation of the lyrics. If you aren't a Spanish speaker, take the time to look up a translation of any lyrics and song titles. You might be surprised at what they mean!

Creating a Harmonic Foundation

Use smooth voice leading to create a seamless harmonic bed for the singer. Avoid abrupt or jarring chord changes that could disrupt the vocal line. Utilise chord inversions to avoid clashing with the melody.

Dynamic Control

Always keep the dynamics in check. The guitar should never overpower the singer but rather complement and enhance the vocal performance. Follow the singer's lead in dynamics, using crescendos and diminuendos to build or release tension along with the vocal line.

Ornamentation and Fills

Add ornaments or fills during pauses or at the ends of phrases but be careful not to overdo it. The focus should remain on the singer. Occasionally, you can echo or lightly harmonise the melody played by the singer to create a richer texture.

Interaction with the Singer

Maintain eye contact with the singer for cues on dynamics, tempo changes, and phrasing. Tango is a collaborative art form, and communication is key. Be prepared to improvise if the singer decides to take liberties with the timing or melody. Flexibility is crucial in live performance settings.

Live Sound Tips

Performing with a nylon-string guitar in a live setting presents unique challenges, especially when it comes to sound amplification and setup. Here are some tips:

Amplification

Consider installing a high-quality pickup system in your guitar. A dual system that combines an under-saddle piezo pickup with an internal microphone can provide a more natural sound that captures the warmth and nuance of a nylon-string guitar. Use a good direct input (DI) box when plugging into a PA system. This ensures a clean signal and can also help with ground loop issues and other electrical noise. A preamp can be useful for controlling tone and volume before the signal reaches the mixer. Look for a preamp with EQ controls tailored for nylon-string guitars.

Microphone Placement

If you prefer to use an external microphone, position it around 6-12 inches from the 12th fret of the guitar. This placement generally captures a balanced tone, avoiding too much bass or treble. For a richer sound, you can blend the sound from an external mic with your guitar's pickup. This method combines the natural resonance of the guitar with the clarity and directness of the pickup. Be aware of your movements on stage if using a mic. Moving too far away from the mic can lead to inconsistent sound levels.

Tone Settings

Start with a flat EQ and make adjustments based on the room's acoustics. Often, cutting some midrange frequencies and slightly boosting the bass and treble can enhance the guitar's natural warmth and clarity. Use reverb sparingly to add depth to your sound. Too much can muddy the tone, especially in a live setting. If you use other effects, such as delay, ensure they complement the natural sound of the guitar.

Monitoring

Ensure you have a clear and accurate monitor mix. In a big ensemble, other instruments can easily drown out nylon-string guitars, so it's important to hear yourself well. If available, in-ear monitors can provide a more controlled and consistent listening experience, particularly in noisy or large venues.

Handling Feedback

Nylon-string guitars are more prone to feedback due to their resonant body. Use feedback suppressors or notch out the problem frequencies with your EQ to control this. A sound hole cover can also help reduce feedback when playing in louder environments. I never leave home without one!

Setup and Environment

Consider using high-tension strings if you need more projection but be aware they require more finger strength. Conversely, medium or low-tension strings can be easier to play and offer a warmer tone, but with less volume. Nylon-string guitars are sensitive to humidity and temperature changes, so ensure the environment where you perform is temperate, as this can affect tuning stability and sound quality. Of course, if this isn't possible… keep a tuner handy!

Backup Gear

In an ideal world we'd always be able to cart around two of everything but, in reality, few of us musicians live in such luxury! If you can, always have spare strings and extra picks if you're using them. If you're in a position to be able to, bring a backup tuner, spare jack lead and a backup DI box or preamp in case of technical issues.

Chapter Ten: Essential Listening

Embarking on the journey to master Tango guitar is much more than acquiring technical skills or memorising chords – it's about immersing yourself in the soul of the music. Tango is a genre rich with history, emotion, and intricate rhythms, which have evolved over the course of more than a century. To truly understand and perform Tango authentically, active listening is indispensable.

In this chapter, we look at the essential recordings every Tango guitarist should know. These are not just songs, they are lessons in the art form – each one offering unique insights into the styles, techniques, and emotional depths of Tango. By studying these works, you'll learn how the greats approached melody, harmony, and rhythm, and how they conveyed profound feelings through their instruments.

From the foundational sounds of early Tango orchestras to the innovative compositions of modern maestros, the recordings selected here will broaden your musical perspective. You'll hear the subtle nuances that define different eras and styles within Tango, and you'll begin to internalise the phrasing and dynamics that make the music so captivating.

Listening is learning. As you explore these essential tracks, pay attention to the guitar's role within each piece: how it interacts with other instruments, supports the vocalist, or takes the spotlight with a solo. Notice the techniques used to create texture and mood and consider how you can add these elements into your own playing.

By the end of this chapter, you'll have a deeper appreciation for the artistry of Tango guitar and a solid foundation of musical references to inspire your continued growth. So put on your headphones, open your mind, and let the music guide you into the heart of Tango.

Early Tango Composers

Carlos Gardel

Recommended Recordings: *El Día Que Me Quieras*; *Mi Buenos Aires Querido*.

Why Listen? Gardel's voice defined Tango singing, and his compositions and recordings set the standard for the genre.

Agustín Bardi

Recommended Recording: *Gallo Ciego (Orquesta Osvaldo Pugliese)*.

Why Listen? Known as one of the fathers of Tango, Bardi's compositions are essential learning for understanding traditional Tango structure and harmony.

Eduardo Arolas

Recommended Recording: *El Marne (Orquesta Juan D'Arienzo)*.

Why Listen? Arolas' work bridges the gap between early Tango and the more sophisticated orchestral arrangements that followed.

Golden Age and Guardia Nueva

Orquesta Juan D'Arienzo

Recommended Recording: *D'Arienzo con Maure VOL.1.*

Why Listen? D'Arienzo was called *Rey del compas* (King of the beat) because of his orchestra's passionate driving rhythms.

Aníbal Troilo

Recommended Recording: *Yo Soy el Tango 1938 – 1941.*

Why Listen? Troilo's orchestra was among the most influential, and his collaborations with guitarist Roberto Grela are legendary.

Roberto Grela

Recommended Recording: *A La Guardia Nueva 1953-1955* (with Aníbal Troilo); *Las Nuevas Creaciones* (Solo).

Why Listen? Grela's guitar work is considered foundational in the evolution of Tango guitar, offering sophisticated phrasing and deep emotional expression.

Quinteto Real

Recommended Recording: *Quinteto Real.*

Why Listen? Quinteto Real played a new genre of a virtuosic Tango created purely for listening rather than dancing.

The New Tango: Piazzolla and Beyond

Astor Piazzolla

Recommended Recordings: *Libertango*; *Oblivion.*

Why Listen? Piazzolla revolutionized Tango, blending it with jazz and classical music. His name has become synonymous with Tango.

Dino Saluzzi

Recommended Recordings: *Cité de la Musique*; *Kultrum.*

Why Listen? Saluzzi's work on the bandoneón often features guitar prominently, creating an atmospheric, experimental style of Tango.

Hugo Díaz

Recommended Recording: *Tangos*.

Why Listen? Hugo Díaz was a harmonica player whose interpretations of Tango standards are unique and often accompanied by superb guitar work.

Tango Guitarists & Specialised Tango Guitar Albums

Hugo Rivas

Recommended Recordings: *Hugo Rivas*; *Tua y Mia* (with Julio Cobelli)

Why Listen? Rivas is known for his virtuosity and deep understanding of traditional Tango, making him a leading contemporary figure in Tango guitar.

Aníbal Arias

Recommended Recording: *Una Guitarra Para Gardel*.

Why Listen? Arias was a technical master and set the standard for virtuosic playing both as a soloist and ensemble performer.

Juanjo Domínguez

Recommended Recording: *Tiempo de Guitarras*.

Why Listen? Domínguez is celebrated for his extraordinary technique and deep interpretations of Tango music, both solo and in ensemble settings.

Troilo Grela by Roberto Grela & Anilbal Troilo.

Why Listen? Some of Grela's best work, showcasing the intricate interplay between guitar and bandoneón.

Tango Suite (Astor Piazzolla) by Sergio & Odair Assad.

Why Listen? This work is a great example of how Tango compositions have become part of the furniture in the classical guitar world. This beautiful arrangement blends Piazzolla's complex compositions with the Assads' stunning guitar work.

Conclusion

In this book, you've taken a journey through the rich and vibrant world of Tango guitar. You've learned the essential chord voicings, rhythmic patterns, and melodic improvisation techniques that form the foundation of this passionate musical style. You've explored the complexities of solo guitar arrangements, the art of accompanying dancers and singers, and embraced the nuances that make Tango compelling and unique.

As you prepare to apply these skills in real-world settings, remember that the essence of Tango lies not just in technical proficiency but in its emotional depth and spontaneity. Tango is more than music – it's an expression of life, filled with joy, sorrow, love and loss. Whether you're performing in a lively *Milonga*, accompanying a soulful singer, or playing solo in a more intimate setting, let the music breathe through your fingers.

Remember that you should embrace the imperfections, the *mugre*, that give Tango its distinctive character. These subtle dissonances and unexpected turns are what make Tango feel alive and authentic.

Learning Tango guitar is a lifelong journey, one that offers opportunities for growth and self-discovery as a musician, and this book is just the beginning. Listen attentively to the great Tango maestros, absorbing their music and artistry.

Connect with other musicians who share your passion. Attend workshops, join ensembles, and participate in jam sessions. Each performance is an opportunity to refine your craft, learn from others, and connect deeply with the music and the community that surrounds it.

Most importantly, enjoy the process. Tango is a music of the heart and soul, and your guitar is the instrument through which you express your voice. Enjoy the moments when the music flows effortlessly and learn from the times when it challenges you.

I hope this book has given you the tools and inspiration you need to express yourself while playing Tango. I look forward to hearing the music you'll create, the stories you'll tell, and the emotions you'll bring to your performance.

Keep playing, keep exploring and, above all, keep the spirit of Tango alive in your music.

¡Viva el Tango!

www.ingramcontent.com/pod-product-compliance
Lightning Source LLC
Chambersburg PA
CBHW081437090426

42740CB00017B/3336